10/13

WILDEBEEST MIGRATION

BY L. E. CARMICHAEL

The Child's World®

Published by The Child's World®
1980 Lookout Drive • Mankato, MN 56003-1705
800-599-READ • www.childsworld.com

ACKNOWLEDGMENTS
The Child's World®: Mary Berendes, Publishing Director
Content Consultant: Dr. Tanya Dewey,
   University of Michigan Museum of Zoology
The Design Lab: Design and production
Red Line Editorial: Editorial direction

PHOTO CREDITS
Juha Sompinmäki/Dreamstime, cover (top), 1, back cover; Stefan Ekernas/
Dreamstime, cover (bottom), 2–3; Stefan Ekernas/Shutterstock Images,
4–5; XNR Productions, 7; Chris Noome/iStockphoto, 8–9; Palenque/
iStockphoto, 10–11; Shutterstock Images, 12; Mike Gatt/iStockphoto, 13;
Morkel Erasmus/Shutterstock Images, 14; Sergey Uryadnikov/Dreamstime,
15; Dreamstime, 16; Paul Banton/iStockphoto, 18; Roman Murushkin/
Dreamstime, 19; David Gomez/iStockphoto, 20; Eric Isselée/Dreamstime,
23; Duncan Noakes/Dreamstime, 24; Anke van Wyk/Bigstock, 26; Nico
Smit/Dreamstime, 28

Design elements: Juha Sompinmäki/Dreamstime

ISBN 9781609736262
LCCN 2011940067

Printed in the United States of America

ABOUT THE AUTHOR: Lindsey E. Carmichael earned a PhD for studying the migration of wolves and arctic foxes in Canada's North. Now she writes nonfiction for children and contributes to the science blog, Sci/Why. She has never seen a wild wildebeest, but once spent half an hour watching a dung beetle work. Lindsey lives in Nova Scotia.

TABLE OF
CONTENTS

WILDEBEESTS

Huge herds of wildebeests live in the grasslands of Africa. There are two different kinds of wildebeest. Black wildebeests live in South Africa, Lesotho, Swaziland, and Namibia. There are about 18,000 in total. Most live on farms where they stay all year.

Blue wildebeests are much more common. They live as far north as Kenya and as far south as South Africa. Some stay in one area all the time. But most blue wildebeests travel. They look for enough food and water to survive.

The blue wildebeests' lifetime journey is their migration. This is when an animal moves from one **habitat** to another. Migrations happen for many reasons. Some animals move to be in warmer weather where there is more food. There they can reproduce or have their babies. And these migrations can be short distances, such as from a mountaintop to its valley. Or they can be long distances, like the wildebeests' journey.

Wildebeests migrate to find food and water.

MIGRATION MAP

Different groups of blue wildebeests migrate in different places. Some migrate in southern Botswana. Some migrate in northern Botswana. Others migrate from Zambia to Angola and back.

The biggest blue wildebeest migration happens in the Serengeti-Mara **Ecosystem**. They move with the seasons. This is **seasonal** migration. In September and October, wildebeests live in the Mara area of Kenya. It is the most northern place they visit. Around November, they start moving south into Tanzania. In March or April, the wildebeests change direction. They travel northwest into the Serengeti National Park. In July or August, they turn northeast and end up back in Kenya. As they move, they go north and south. This is **latitudinal** migration.

This map shows wildebeest migration through the Serengeti-Mara Ecosystem.

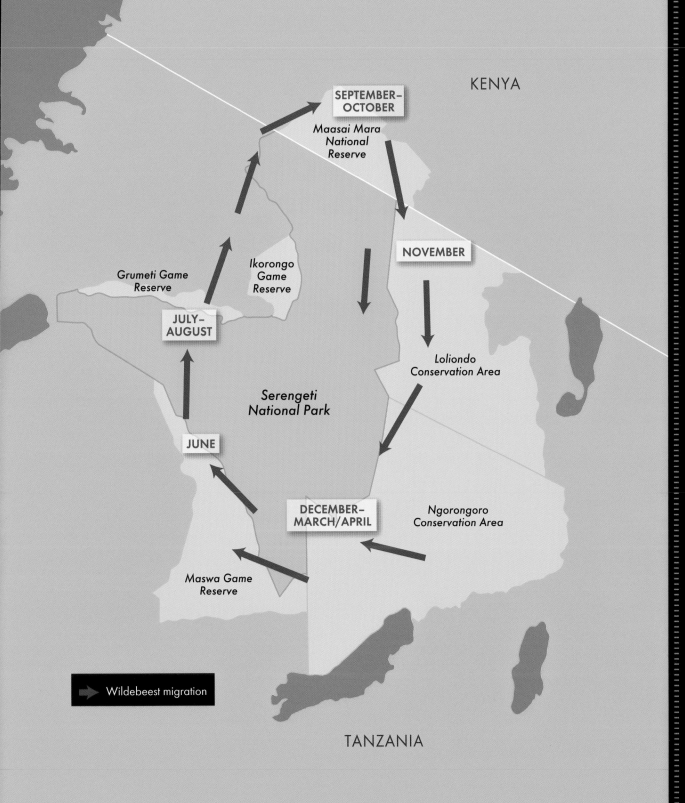

KENYA

SEPTEMBER–
OCTOBER

*Maasai Mara
National
Reserve*

NOVEMBER

*Ikorongo
Game
Reserve*

*Grumeti Game
Reserve*

*Loliondo
Conservation Area*

JULY–
AUGUST

*Serengeti
National Park*

JUNE

DECEMBER–
MARCH/APRIL

*Ngorongoro
Conservation Area*

*Maswa Game
Reserve*

➡ Wildebeest migration

TANZANIA

CLOWNS OF THE SAVANNA

Blue wildebeests look like they are made from spare parts. They have horns, hooves, and long **muzzles**. They have tails like horses. Their front halves look too big for their back ends. Wildebeest fur is gray with shiny silver. That is why they are called blue.

An African name for wildebeest is gnu. This is the sound a wildebeest makes. Wildebeests look and sound funny. Some people call them the clowns of the **savanna**.

Male wildebeests are bulls. Females are cows. Their babies are calves. There are 1.55 million blue wildebeests in Africa. Of these, 1.2 million live in the Serengeti-Mara Ecosystem. These wildebeests migrate with 200,000 zebras and 350,000 gazelles. It is the biggest **mammal** migration in the world.

Wildebeests look like a mix of animals.

THE SERENGETI-MARA ECOSYSTEM

Several parts of Africa make up the Serengeti-Mara Ecosystem. The first is Serengeti National Park, in Tanzania. Southwest of the Serengeti is the Maswa Game **Reserve**. And southeast of the Serengeti is the Ngorongoro Conservation Area. In the north is the Maasai Mara Wildlife Reserve in Kenya. The land in this reserve is set aside for animals and plants. People cannot hunt or farm there.

The Maasai people of Africa call the ecosystem *Siringitu*. This means "the place where the land moves on forever." Very few trees live here. Most of the trees grow by the rivers. Everywhere else is grassy savanna. Different grasses grow in different areas. The grass in the Ngorongoro is shorter than the grass in the Serengeti.

The Serengeti-Mara Ecosystem covers 25,000 square miles (40,000 sq km). Elephants, antelope, ostriches, hyenas, lions, cheetahs, and monkeys live there. But the parks were made for the **grazers** that migrate, such as zebras and gazelles. A very important grazer is the wildebeest.

Many of Earth's wildebeests live in the Serengeti-Mara.

THE WET SEASON

Africa has two main seasons. They are the dry season and the wet season. It hardly ever rains in the dry season. The ground gets hard. The plants turn brown. Wildebeests need to drink every one or two days. They usually stay near water sources, such as lakes and rivers. By the end of the dry season, the animals have eaten all of the grass by the water. Wildebeests must travel as far as 30 miles (50 km) to find food.

In the wet season, storms come to the savanna. Thunder rumbles. Rain pours down. Water collects on the ground. Grass sprouts in a few days. This makes everything green. This soft, fresh grass is the perfect food for wildebeests. The grass grows as long as the rain keeps falling.

The wet season lasts from about November to May. Wildebeests spend this time in Ngorongoro. This area is near a volcano. The soil is full of **nutrients**. They make the grass very healthy. When it is raining, there is also water for wildebeests to drink.

In the wet season, storms turn the savanna green.

Wildebeests move from one patch of grass to another. They like to graze in groups. Mothers and calves stay with other mothers and calves. Calves form their own groups when they are eight months old. Young females stay with other cows. Young males graze with other bulls.

The herds travel back and forth across the Ngorongoro. They feed here until it stops raining. This is usually in May. Then the water disappears and the grass dries up. But, it is still raining in the Serengeti. The wildebeests start to migrate west.

Mothers and calves stay in groups together.

MOVING AND MATING

Wildebeests have scent patches in their front hooves. They leave a scent trail when they walk. Wildebeests migrate with their heads close to the ground. They sniff out the trail of the animals in front. The herds travel in single file. There are many lines and many animals. The wildebeests look like rivers flowing across the savanna.

While they move, wildebeests also mate in mating season. Mating starts in late May or early June. Each bull creates a **territory**. This is land he will not let other males enter. He uses his scent to mark the territory. Then bulls chase cows into their territories.

Wildebeests move in a long line across the savanna.

A LINE OF MIGRATING WILDEBEESTS CAN BE UP TO 12.5 MILES (20 KM) LONG.

Males try to keep other bulls from stealing their mates. They chase the bulls away or fight them. When two males fight, they kneel on their front legs. Then they hit and push each other with their horns. Their horns crash together. The bulls make loud cries.

Mating lasts about two weeks. Before it ends, most of the wildebeest cows will mate. Many cows are still nursing calves that are a few months old. Their new babies will be born after eight months.

Bulls fight each other during mating season.

CROSSING THE RIVER

Wildebeests travel northwest until July. There is less rain now. The Serengeti is getting dry. Wildebeests change direction. They head for the Maasai Mara Reserve. Rain is still falling there. They have to cross the Mara River to get there. Danger waits for the animals at the river.

The wildebeests must cross this river, though. The southern part of the Serengeti gets only 20 inches (500 mm) of rain all year. Once the rain stops, the plants die. The grasslands turn into desert. There is nowhere for wildebeests to drink. The Mara area gets 47 inches (1200 mm) of rain per year. In the dry season, wildebeests can find food and water there.

Wildebeests move toward the Maasai Mara in July.

The Mara River is fast and wide. Wet season rains make it deep. The wildebeests arrive from all over the Serengeti plains. They pile up on the riverbank. They try to decide where to cross. The animals at the back push the animals in the front. Finally, the leaders jump in. They swim hard for the other side.

The Mara River is full of crocodiles. They attack many wildebeests. Others die because they panic. They climb over each other. Some wildebeests are hurt or drown. There is more danger on the other side of the river. Lions and hyenas hide in the trees. They hunt wildebeests that are too tired to get away. Sometimes calves lose their mothers. They run along the banks and call out. If they cannot find their mothers, they will be killed, too.

Wildebeests leap into the Mara River.

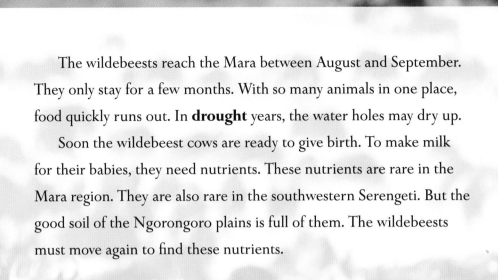

The wildebeests reach the Mara between August and September. They only stay for a few months. With so many animals in one place, food quickly runs out. In **drought** years, the water holes may dry up.

Soon the wildebeest cows are ready to give birth. To make milk for their babies, they need nutrients. These nutrients are rare in the Mara region. They are also rare in the southwestern Serengeti. But the good soil of the Ngorongoro plains is full of them. The wildebeests must move again to find these nutrients.

Lions attack wildebeests on the other side of the river.

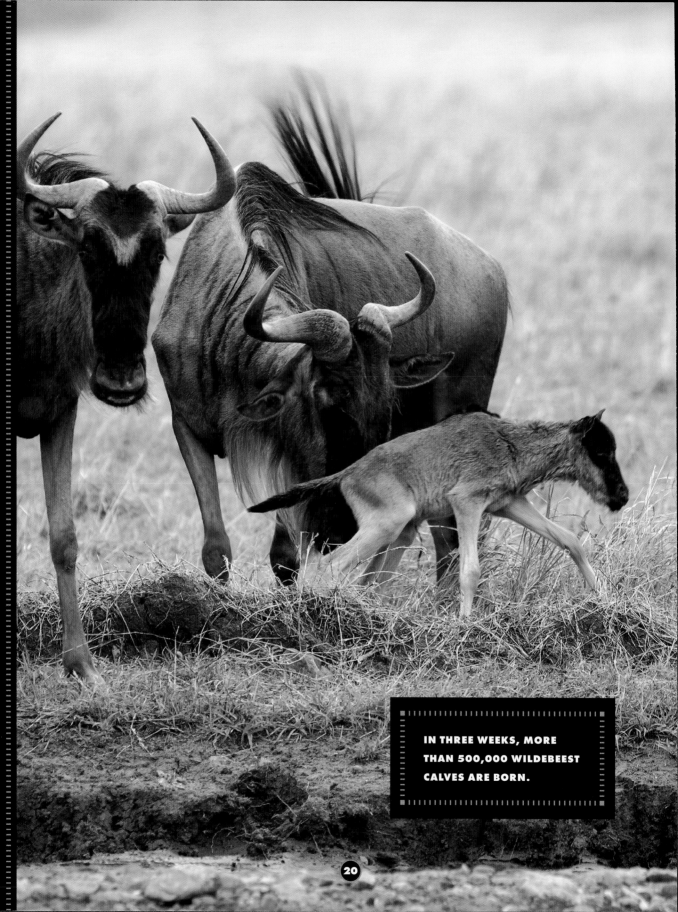

IN THREE WEEKS, MORE THAN 500,000 WILDEBEEST CALVES ARE BORN.

CALVING SEASON

The dry season usually ends around October or November. The wildebeests see thunderstorms to the south. They know to move again. They head for the Ngorongoro plains. They arrive just in time for calving season.

When calves are born, they try to stand up right away. The calf is on its feet in less than ten minutes. Calves quickly begin to nurse. They can follow their mothers in just a few hours.

Each cow stays close to her calf for the first few days. This gives the calf time to **imprint**. The calf knows which animal is its mother. Wildebeests know each other by scent and sounds.

Most calves are born over three weeks. Scientists call this **swamping**. Lions try to hunt calves because adult wildebeests are harder to catch. At calving season, lions can eat so many calves that they quickly get full. When lions are hungry again, the calves are bigger. They are harder to hunt.

There are 2,500 lions in the Serengeti-Mara Ecosystem. These lions stay inside their territories. The migrating wildebeests are always on the move. Lions do not follow the wildebeests as they move on.

Calves stand soon after they are born.

CHASING THE RAINS

Calves are born in January or February. That is when the wet season starts. The wildebeests stay in the Ngorongoro area until the rains end. The mothers have time to eat the healthy grasses. The calves have time to drink their mothers' milk. The calves grow strong enough to join the migration.

Mating season comes again. By now, the wildebeests have traveled more than 930 miles (1,500 km). In good, wet years, their trip is shorter. In drought years, they have to travel farther for food and water. The longest wildebeest migration scientists have measured was more than 1,988 miles (3,200 km).

Wildebeests do not migrate in a straight path from one place to another. They might walk back and forth or go in small circles. They take different paths in different years. But they always move between the Ngorongoro, the Serengeti, and the Mara. How do they find their way? Wildebeests can see, hear, and smell rainstorms. Wildebeests may also feel changes in the water in the air. Scientists have seen wildebeests walk toward storms up to 60 miles (100 km) away. Some people say that the wildebeests do not migrate. Instead, they chase the rains.

Wildebeests follow the rains as they migrate.

AN IMPORTANT SPECIES

Migration is very important to wildebeests. It helps them find the right habitat for every season. They get the nutrients they need all year long. It also helps them protect their calves from **predators**.

Wildebeest migration is also important for the Serengeti-Mara Ecosystem. That is because wildebeests are an important **species** in the savanna ecosystem.

WILDEBEESTS IN THE SERENGETI-MARA ECOSYSTEM MAKE 420 TONS (375 TONNES) OF DUNG EVERY DAY.

Wildebeests turn grass into dung. The ecosystem would not exist without dung. The dung has to be buried to help the soil. Dung beetles do that job. Dung beetles are born underground. They climb out of the earth and follow wildebeests. They use scent to find them. The beetles can find wildebeests up to 6 miles (10 km) away. The beetles find fresh wildebeest dung. They roll it into small balls. They dig holes and bury the dung in the ground. Female beetles lay one egg on each dung ball. When the eggs hatch, new beetles find more wildebeest dung. The beetles bury dung in the wet season. This is when the ground is soft.

This dung contains nutrients for grasses. It makes the grasses grow. The beetles dig holes to bury the dung. This loosens the soil. It also lets air into the soil. With the help of dung beetles, wildebeests give nutrients to the grass they eat for food.

Wildebeests trample and kill small tree seedlings. In the mating season, bulls use their horns to slash at larger trees. This kills the trees before they can take over the grasslands. This helps the wildebeests' habitat. Many other grazers use this habitat, such as zebras and antelope.

Wildebeests provide food for animals in other ways, too. Thomson's gazelles graze where wildebeests have already eaten. And wildebeests are food for lions, crocodiles, and other savanna predators.

Dung beetles use wildebeest dung, which helps the savanna ecosystem.

Crop field fences can stop wildebeests from getting to water.

IN 1973, A FENCE WAS BUILT AROUND ETOSHA NATIONAL PARK IN BOTSWANA. THE FENCE STOPPED 30,000 WILDEBEESTS FROM MIGRATING DURING THE DRY SEASON. BY 1993, ONLY 2,000 WILDEBEESTS WERE LEFT IN THE PARK.

WILDEBEESTS AT RISK

There are 1.55 million blue wildebeests in Africa. It seems impossible they could ever become **endangered**. But, blue wildebeests face many threats.

Wildebeests need the Mara region of Kenya to survive the dry season. This important habitat is changing. Droughts happen more often. They last longer, too. Scientists guess that **climate** change is making this happen. Earth's temperatures are getting warmer. Gases are being trapped in the air. Climate change makes the weather change. Less rain may fall. Wildebeests need rain to survive. In drought years, it is harder for them to find enough to eat and drink. More animals die.

Another danger is that many parts of Kenya are not safe for wildebeests. In these places, farms are a threat. Cows on farms want to eat the same food that wildebeests eat. Cows need water, too. This means there is less food and water for wildebeests. People turn grasslands into wheat fields. Wildebeests cannot graze in farmers' fields. Farmers may kill wildebeests that wander onto their land.

Fences may be the biggest threat to wildebeests. In Africa, people build fences for many reasons. Farmers use them to keep wildlife out of their fields. Fences stop diseases from spreading to cows. They also keep hunters away from wildlife.

Many people do not understand that fences harm wildebeests. Fences can stop wildebeests from getting to water. Wildebeests die because of the fences. In some areas, as many as nine out of every ten wildebeests have died in just 20 years.

Scientists worry about the Serengeti-Mara wildebeests. Many come within 6 miles (10 km) or closer to the edges of the park. Sometimes, wildebeests travel outside of the reserve. This happens in two places. One is the Ikoma Open Area. The other is the Mara Group Ranches. People can hunt wildebeests there. In the future, people could farm or build fences. If wildebeests cannot travel through these areas, they might not be able to migrate. If they cannot migrate, the Serengeti-Mara wildebeests will begin to die.

Most blue wildebeests on Earth live in the Serengeti-Mara. Without this population, the whole species could disappear. If this happens, other animals living in these areas could disappear, too. Scientists are working to make sure wildebeest populations remain. With the right help from others, wildebeests can continue to migrate across the African savanna.

Wildebeest migration is important to the African savanna.

TYPES OF MIGRATION

Different animals migrate for different reasons. Some move because of the climate. Some travel to find food or a mate. Here are the different types of animal migration:

Seasonal migration: This type of migration happens when the seasons change. Most animals migrate for this reason. Other types of migration, such as altitudinal and latitudinal, may also include seasonal migration.

Latitudinal migration: When animals travel north and south, it is called latitudinal migration. Doing so allows animals to change the climate where they live.

Altitudinal migration: This migration happens when animals move up and down mountains. In summer, animals can live higher on a mountain. During the cold winter, they move down to lower and warmer spots.

Reproductive migration: Sometimes animals move to have their babies. This migration may keep the babies safer when they are born. Or babies may need a certain habitat to live in after birth.

Nomadic migration: Animals may wander from place to place to find food in this type of migration.

Complete migration: This type of migration happens when animals are finished mating in an area. Then almost all of the animals leave the area. They may travel more than 15,000 miles (25,000 km) to spend winters in a warmer area.

Partial migration: When some, but not all, animals of one type move away from their mating area, it is partial migration. This is the most common type of migration.

Irruptive migration: This type of migration may happen one year, but not the next. It may include some or all of a type of animal. And the animal group may travel short or long distances.

SOMETIMES ANIMALS NEVER COME BACK TO A PLACE WHERE THEY ONCE LIVED. THIS CAN HAPPEN WHEN HUMANS OR NATURE DESTROY THEIR HABITAT. FOOD, WATER, OR SHELTER MAY BECOME HARD TO FIND. OR A GROUP OF ANIMALS MAY BECOME TOO LARGE FOR AN AREA. THEN THEY MUST MOVE TO FIND FOOD.

GLOSSARY

climate (KLYE-mit): The climate is the usual weather in a place. Climate change can affect wildebeests.

drought (DROUT): A drought is a long time of dry weather. Rain is hard to find in a drought.

dung (DUNG): Dung is an animal's waste matter. Dung is used by beetles in the savanna.

ecosystem (EE-koh-siss-tuhm): An ecosystem is a community of plants and animals that depend on each other and the land. Each animal is important to the ecosystem.

endangered (en-DAYN-jurd): An animal is endangered when it is at risk of disappearing forever. Many animals are at risk of becoming endangered.

grazers (GRAYZ-urz): Grazers are animals that eat grass for food. Wildebeests and zebras are grazers.

habitat (HAB-uh-tat): A habitat is a place that has the food, water, and shelter an animal needs to survive. Wildebeests change their habitat as they migrate.

imprint (IM-print): To imprint is to fix in the memory. Calves imprint their mothers' smells and sounds.

latitudinal (LAT-uh-tood-i-nul): Latitudinal relates to how far north and south something is from the equator. Wildebeests have a latitudinal migration.

mammal (MAM-uhl): A mammal is a warm-blooded animal whose females make milk for their young. A wildebeest is a mammal.

muzzles (MUHZ-ulz): Muzzles are animals' noses, mouths, and jaws. Wildebeests have long muzzles.

nutrients (NOO-tree-untz): Nutrients are things that people, animals, and plants need to stay alive. Soil by a volcano has many nutrients for the wildebeest.

predators (PRED-uh-turs): Predators are animals that hunt and eat other animals. Lions are predators of wildebeest calves.

reserve (ri-ZURV): A reserve is a place that is set aside to keep animals and plants safe. The Serengeti-Mara is a large reserve.

savanna (suh-VAN-uh): A savanna is a flat, grassy area with few or no trees. The savanna has grasses wildebeests eat.

seasonal (SEE-zuhn-uhl): Seasonal is something related to the seasons of the year. Wildebeests follow the rain on their seasonal migration.

species (SPEE-sheez): A species is a group of animals that are similar in certain ways. Some species help the environment in big ways.

swamping (SWAHMP-ing): Swamping is when a group of animals have their babies around the same time each year. Swamping helps more calves live each year.

territory (TER-uh-tor-ee): A territory is the land that one animal marks for its own. A bull marks his territory with scent.

FURTHER INFORMATION

Books

Catt, Thessaly. *Migrating with the Wildebeest.*
New York: PowerKids Press, 2011.

Cole, Melissa S. *Wildebeests.* San Diego:
Blackbirch Press, 2002.

Levy, Janey. *World Habitats: Discovering the
Tropical Savanna.* New York: Rosen, 2008.

Web Sites

Visit our Web site for links about wildebeest
migration: *childsworld.com/links*

Note to Parents, Teachers, and Librarians:
We routinely verify our Web links to make sure
they are safe and active sites. So encourage
your readers to check them out!

INDEX